student cookbook

introduction

So, you've finally done it. You've left home, struck out on your own. Well done: you've become a student. The hallowed halls and dreaming spires of academia are calling, a wide world of learning beckons. Well, something like that, anyway. Going to university is not just about libraries, laboratories and lectures – let's face it, if it was, then the experience wouldn't be half as much fun. No: the real point of student life is what happens when you're away from your books. In short, you're going to have the time of your life. You're independent now – nobody's going to tell you what time to get up or go to bed, nobody's going to dictate where and how often you go out... and nobody's going to tell you what to eat.

You do have some responsibilities, of course. Living on a budget is never easy, coping with doing your own washing can take a bit of practice, and, given why you're there in the first place, some studying may even have to be done. And, of course, amidst the general madness of student life, you're going to have to eat. Not only eat – you're going to have to cook. It's tricky, we know. When you've got so much to do,

student cookbook
100 everyday recipes

First published in 2011
LOVE FOOD is an imprint of Parragon Books Ltd

Parragon
Queen Street House
4 Queen Street
Bath BA1 1HE, UK

ISBN: 978-1-4454-4714-8

Printed in China

Produced by Ivy Contract
Cover photography by Mike Cooper
Cover image home economy and food styling by Lincoln Jefferson

Notes for the Reader

This book uses both metric and imperial measurements. Follow the same units of measurement throughout; do not mix metric and imperial. All spoon measurements are level: teaspoons are assumed to be 5 ml, and tablespoons are assumed to be 15 ml. Unless otherwise stated, milk is assumed to be full fat, eggs and individual vegetables are medium, and pepper is freshly ground black pepper.

The times given are an approximate guide only. Preparation times differ according to the techniques used by different people and the cooking times may also vary from those given. Optional ingredients, variations or serving suggestions have not been included in the calculations.

Recipes using raw or very lightly cooked eggs should be avoided by infants, the elderly, pregnant women, convalescents and anyone suffering from an illness. Pregnant and breastfeeding women are advised to avoid eating peanuts and peanut products. Sufferers from nut allergies should be aware that some of the ready-made ingredients used in the recipes in this book may contain nuts. Always check the packaging before use.

Vegetarians should be aware that some of the ready-made ingredients used in the recipes in this book may contain animal products. Always check the packaging before use.

taking the time out to prepare gourmet-quality meals can seem a pretty low priority. And blowing your hard-earned student loan on anything more nutritious than a take-away burger can seem like pure wanton extravagance. But it needn't be so. There can be so much more to student cooking than ketchup pasta and cheesy chips. Putting together fresh, wholesome meals can be fast, easy and, most importantly, cheap.

Learning to cook for yourself is not only healthier than a diet of take-aways and ready meals, it's easier on the overdraft too. For the cost of a couple of microwave curries and a late-night kebab you can eat fresh food for a week. Getting stuck into the kitchen can be a great way to unwind at the end of the day; it can be a fantastic means of socializing with your fellow house- or hall-mates and it's a pretty reliable way of impressing any potential dates. And, of course, knowing you're eating properly will give your parents one less thing to worry about. And most of all, it's fun! So grab an apron, open up these pages and tuck in. Trust us: there's really nothing like a bit of home cooking for finally shaking that 14-hour hangover...

the big breakfast

fruity yogurt with granola

ingredients

serves 1

200 g/7 oz rolled oats
2 tbsp clear honey
2 tbsp pumpkin seeds
2 tbsp sunflower seeds
2 tbsp chopped walnuts
1 small ripe pear, peeled,
    cored and chopped
½ ripe mango, peeled, stoned
    and chopped
125 g/4½ oz natural yogurt

method

1 Preheat the oven to 180°C/350°F/Gas Mark 4.

2 For the granola, mix the oats and honey together in a bowl and spread out on a baking sheet. Bake in the preheated oven for 10–15 minutes, stirring a couple of times, until the oats are lightly browned, then remove from the oven and leave to cool.

3 Place the seeds in a mortar and briefly grind with a pestle to break them into smaller pieces. Mix with the cooled oats and the walnuts.

4 To assemble, put half the pear and mango in a glass and top with half the yogurt and a spoonful of granola. Repeat with the remaining fruit and yogurt and top with more granola.

mango smoothie

ingredients
serves 1

1 ripe mango, peeled,
    stoned and sliced
1 tsp clear honey
200 ml/7 fl oz freshly squeezed
    orange juice
2 tbsp natural yogurt

method

1 Put the mango, honey, orange juice and yogurt into a tall beaker.

2 Using a hand-held stick blender, process until smooth.

3 Pour into a glass and serve immediately.

fruity porridge

ingredients

serves 4

175 g/6 oz jumbo porridge oats
55 g/2 oz oatmeal
pinch of salt (optional)
850 ml/1½ pints milk
55 g/2 oz ready-to-eat dried
    apricots, chopped
25 g/1 oz sunflower seeds
2 bananas, sliced

method.

1 Place the oats and oatmeal in a saucepan together with
  the salt, if using, and stir in the milk. Place over a gentle
  heat and cook, stirring, for 7–8 minutes, or until the
  oats thicken.

2 Stir the apricots and sunflower seeds into the pan, then
  spoon into individual dishes and top with the sliced
  banana and serve.

banana breakfast shake

ingredients

serves 2

2 ripe bananas, chopped
200 ml/7 fl oz low-fat natural
    yogurt
125 ml/4 fl oz milk
½ tsp vanilla extract
honey, for drizzling

method

1 Put the bananas, yogurt, milk and vanilla extract into a tall beaker.

2 Using a hand-held stick blender, process until smooth.

3 Pour into glasses, drizzle with honey and serve the banana shake immediately.

melon & strawberry crunch

ingredients
serves 4

25 g/1 oz rolled oats
25 g/1 oz oat bran
2 tbsp toasted flaked almonds
25 g/1 oz ready-to-eat dried
    apricots, finely chopped
½ melon, such as Galia
225 g/8 oz strawberries, hulled
150 ml/5 fl oz milk or orange juice,
    to serve

method

1 Put the rolled oats and oat bran in a bowl and stir in the almonds and dried apricots.

2 Discard the skin and seeds from the melon and cut into small bite-sized pieces. Halve the strawberries if large.

3 Divide the rolled oat mixture between 4 individual bowls, then top with the melon and strawberries. Serve with either milk or orange juice.

grilled cinnamon oranges

ingredients

serves 4

2 large oranges
1 tsp ground cinnamon
1 tbsp demerara sugar

method

1 Cut the oranges in half and discard any pips. Using a sharp knife or a curved grapefruit knife, carefully cut the flesh away from the skin by cutting around the edge of the fruit. Cut across the segments to loosen the flesh into bite-sized pieces that will then spoon out easily.

2 Arrange the orange halves, cut-side up, in a shallow ovenproof dish. Mix the cinnamon with the sugar in a small bowl and sprinkle evenly over the orange halves.

3 Preheat the grill to high. Grill the orange halves for 3–5 minutes, or until the sugar has caramelized and is golden and bubbling. Serve immediately.

citrus zinger

ingredients

serves 1

1 pink grapefruit
1 orange
½ lemon
½ lime
lime slice, to decorate

method

1 Cut the grapefruit and orange in half using a sharp knife.

2 Using a lemon squeezer, juice the grapefruit, orange, lemon and lime and pour into a glass. Stir, decorate with a lime slice and serve immediately.

cinnamon apples on fruit toast

ingredients
serves 1

1 tbsp unsalted butter
½ tsp ground cinnamon
1 apple, cored and sliced
1 slice fruit bread
golden syrup, to serve

method

1 Melt the butter in a saucepan over a low heat and stir in the cinnamon. Add the apple and stir well to coat.

2 Preheat the grill and line the grill pan with foil. Spread the buttered apple over the grill pan. Grill until the apple is just beginning to brown.

3 Toast the fruit bread and serve with the apple piled on top, drizzled with a little golden syrup.

french toast

ingredients

serves 2

2 slices 2-day old white bread
100 ml/3½ fl oz milk
1 egg
pinch of salt
2 tbsp unsalted butter
½ tsp ground cinnamon
1 tsp granulated sugar

method

1 Slice the bread in half diagonally and place, in a single layer, in a shallow dish. Pour over the milk and leave to soak for 1–2 minutes, then turn over the bread.

2 Place the egg and salt in a bowl and beat well. Dip the soaked bread slices into the egg mix.

3 Heat the butter in a frying pan until it foams, then add the bread slices. Cook the French toast until golden brown on both sides. Drain on kitchen paper, then transfer to serving plates.

4 Mix together the cinnamon and sugar in a small bowl, then sprinkle over the French toast. Serve immediately.

apple pancakes with maple syrup butter

ingredients
serves 4–6

200 g/7 oz self-raising flour
100 g/3½ oz caster sugar
1 tsp ground cinnamon
1 egg
200 ml/7 fl oz milk
2 apples, peeled and grated
1 tsp butter
apple wedges, to serve

maple syrup butter

85 g/3 oz butter, softened
3 tbsp maple syrup

method

1 To make the pancakes, mix the flour, sugar and cinnamon together in a bowl and make a well in the centre. Beat the egg and the milk together and pour into the well. Using a wooden spoon, gently incorporate the dry ingredients into the liquid, then stir in the grated apple.

2 Heat the butter in a large non-stick frying pan over a low heat until bubbling. Add tablespoons of the pancake mixture to form 9-cm/3½-inch circles. Cook each pancake for about 1 minute, until it starts to bubble lightly on the top and looks set, then flip it over and cook the other side for 30 seconds, or until cooked through. The pancakes should be golden brown; if not, increase the heat a little. Remove from the pan and keep warm. Repeat the process until all of the pancake batter has been used up.

3 To make the maple syrup butter, melt the butter with the maple syrup in a saucepan over a low heat and stir until combined. To serve, place the pancakes on serving dishes and spoon over the flavoured butter. Serve warm with apple wedges.

fruity muffins

ingredients

makes 10

280 g/10 oz self-raising
  wholemeal flour
2 tsp baking powder
2 tbsp dark muscovado sugar
100 g/3½ oz ready-to-eat dried
  apricots, finely chopped
1 banana, mashed with 1 tbsp
  orange juice
1 tsp finely grated orange rind
300 ml/10 fl oz milk
1 egg, beaten
3 tbsp sunflower oil
2 tbsp rolled oats

method

1 Preheat the oven to 200°C/400°F/Gas Mark 6. Place
  10 paper muffin cases in a muffin tin.

2 Sift the flour and baking powder into a mixing bowl,
  adding any husks that remain in the sieve. Stir in the
  sugar and apricots.

3 Make a well in the centre and add the banana, orange
  rind, milk, egg and oil. Stir gently to form a thick batter
  and divide between the muffin cases.

4 Sprinkle over the oats and bake in the preheated oven
  for 25–30 minutes, until well risen and firm to the
  touch or until a cocktail stick inserted into the centre
  comes out clean.

5 Remove the muffins from the oven and put them on
  a wire rack to cool slightly. Serve the muffins while
  still warm.

blueberry bliss

ingredients

serves 2

250 g/9 oz fresh or frozen
   blueberries
500 g/1 lb 2 oz vanilla-flavoured
   yogurt
½ large banana, chopped
lemon juice or honey, to taste

method

1 Put the blueberries, yogurt and banana into a
   tall beaker.

2 Using a hand-held stick blender, process until smooth.

3 Add a little lemon juice or honey to taste, then process
   again. Pour the blueberry shake into tall glasses and
   serve immediately.

ham & cheese croissant

ingredients

serves 1

1 croissant
1 egg, hard-boiled and sliced
2 thin slices cooked ham, halved
mustard, to taste (optional)
about 25 g/1 oz or 2 slices hard
    cheese, such as Cheddar,
    Gruyère or Emmenthal

method

1 Preheat the grill to medium–high. Slice the croissant horizontally in half, then lay it, cut-sides up, on the rack in the grill pan.

2 Top each croissant half with half the hard-boiled egg and a slice of ham, and spread with a little mustard, if using. Top with the cheese slices, cutting and overlapping them to fit the croissant. Cook under the preheated grill for about 2 minutes, until the cheese has melted. The croissant will be warmed through and beginning to brown around the edges.

3 Invert the top half of the croissant on top of the bottom half. Serve immediately.

chive scrambled eggs

ingredients

serves 2

4 eggs
100 ml/3½ fl oz single cream
2 tbsp snipped fresh chives,
    plus extra to garnish
25 g/1 oz butter
4 slices bread
salt and pepper

method

1 Break the eggs into a medium bowl and whisk gently with the cream. Season to taste with salt and pepper and add the snipped chives.

2 Melt the butter in a frying pan and pour in the egg mixture. Leave to set slightly, then move the mixture towards the centre of the pan using a wooden spoon as the eggs begin to cook. Continue in this way until the eggs are cooked but still creamy.

3 Lightly toast the bread in a toaster or under the grill and place on plates. Spoon over the scrambled eggs, garnish with chives and serve immediately.

sunshine toast

ingredients

serves 1

1 slice granary or wholemeal
bread
1 tbsp olive oil
2–3 mushrooms, sliced
1 tomato, halved
1 small egg
pepper

method

1 Preheat the grill to medium. Very lightly toast the bread under the grill. Using a biscuit cutter, cut a hole in the centre of the slice of toast, large enough to hold the egg.

2 Heat the oil in a non-stick frying pan and cook the mushrooms and tomato, cut-sides down, for 3–4 minutes, until the mushrooms are beginning to brown. Turn the tomato over.

3 Make a space in the middle of the pan and add the toast. Crack the egg open and carefully pour it into the hole in the toast. Reduce the heat and cook slowly until cooked through.

4 Season to taste with pepper, then transfer the toast, mushrooms and tomato to a serving plate.

potato cakes with bacon & eggs

ingredients

serves 4

450 g/1 lb large potatoes, peeled
5 eggs
3 tbsp plain flour
3 tbsp sunflower oil
8 rashers bacon
6 cherry tomatoes, halved
salt and pepper

method

1 Grate the potatoes, rinse in a colander, then spread out on a clean tea towel. Gather up the sides and squeeze to remove any water.

2 Beat 1 of the eggs in a large bowl. Add the potatoes, flour, and salt and pepper to taste and stir well. Take handfuls of the potato mixture and form into round patties about 7 cm/2¾ inches across. Heat 2 tablespoons of the oil in a frying pan. Cook the potato cakes, in batches, for 5 minutes on each side, until golden. Drain on kitchen paper and keep wam.

3 Preheat the grill to medium–high. Grill the bacon for 8 minutes, turning once, until crisp. Grill the tomatoes for 2–3 minutes.

4 Meanwhile, add the remaining oil to the frying pan and fry the remaining eggs for 5 minutes, until the white is set.

5 Transfer the potato cakes, bacon, tomatoes and eggs to plates and serve immediately.

breakfast omelette

ingredients

serves 4

4 pork or vegetarian sausages
small knob of butter
2 tsp sunflower oil, plus extra
    if necessary
12 cherry tomatoes
6 eggs, beaten
salt and pepper

method

1 Preheat the grill to medium–high. Line the grill pan with foil. Arrange the sausages on the grill rack and grill, turning frequently, until cooked through and golden all over. Leave to cool slightly, then cut into bite-sized pieces.

2 Meanwhile, melt the butter with the oil in a medium-sized frying pan with a heatproof handle and cook the tomatoes, turning occasionally, for 2 minutes.

3 Add the sausage pieces so that they are evenly distributed in the base of the frying pan among the tomatoes. Add a little more oil if the frying pan appears dry.

4 Season the eggs to taste with salt and pepper and pour over the sausages and tomatoes. Cook for 3 minutes, without stirring, then place the pan under the grill and cook the top for 3 minutes, or until set and lightly golden. Cut into wedges to serve.

baked eggs with ham & tomato

ingredients

serves 1

1 tsp olive oil
½ small leek, chopped
2 slices wafer-thin ham,
    chopped
1 egg
25 g/1 oz Cheddar cheese,
    grated
2 slices tomato

method

1 Preheat the oven to 180°C/350°F/Gas Mark 4.

2 Heat the oil in a saucepan and cook the leek for 5–6 minutes, until soft.

3 Place the leek in the bottom of a ramekin and top with the ham. Crack and pour in the egg, then top with the cheese and tomato.

4 Bake in the preheated oven for 10 minutes, until the egg is set. Remove the ramekin from the oven, leave to cool a little and serve.

eggs benedict

ingredients

serves 4

1 tbsp white wine vinegar
4 eggs
4 English muffins
4 slices ham

quick hollandaise sauce

3 egg yolks, beaten
200 g/7 oz butter
1 tbsp lemon juice
pepper

method

1 To poach the eggs, fill a frying pan three-quarters full with water and bring to the boil over a low heat. Reduce the heat to a simmer and add the vinegar. When the water is barely simmering, carefully break the eggs into the frying pan. Poach the eggs for 3 minutes, or until the whites are just set but the yolks are still soft.

2 Meanwhile, to make the hollandaise sauce, place the egg yolks in a blender or food processor. Melt the butter in a small saucepan until bubbling. With the motor running, gradually add the hot butter to the blender in a steady stream until the sauce is thick and creamy. Add the lemon juice, and a little warm water if the sauce is too thick, then season to taste with pepper. Remove from the blender or food processor and keep warm.

3 Preheat the grill to medium. Split the muffins and toast them on both sides. To serve, top each muffin with a slice of ham, a poached egg and a generous spoonful of hollandaise sauce.

grab & go

tex-mex roll-ups

ingredients
serves 2

2 flour tortillas
2 tbsp baked beans, mashed
2 tbsp grated Cheddar cheese
2–3 tbsp cooked chicken, finely
    chopped or shredded
1 tomato, sliced
¼ avocado, peeled and cut
    into strips

method

1 Put each tortilla on a microwavable plate. Spread the beans over each tortilla and sprinkle with the cheese. Microwave for about 15 seconds until the cheese melts. Leave to cool slightly.

2 Arrange the chicken, tomato and avocado on top. Roll up and cut into small pieces. Wrap in foil for a packed lunch.

tortillas with tuna, egg & sweetcorn

ingredients

serves 2

1 large egg, hard-boiled
    and cooled
200 g/7 oz canned tuna, drained
200 g/7 oz canned sweetcorn
    kernels, drained
2 flour tortillas
1 punnet mustard cress

dressing

1 tbsp natural yogurt
1 tsp olive oil
½ tsp white wine vinegar
½ tsp Dijon mustard
pepper

method

1 To make the dressing, whisk the yogurt, oil, vinegar, mustard and pepper to taste in a jug until emulsified and smooth.

2 Shell the egg, separate the yolk and the white, then mash the yolk and chop the white finely. Mash the tuna with the egg and dressing, then mix in the sweetcorn.

3 Spread the filling equally over the 2 tortillas and sprinkle over the mustard cress. Fold in one end and roll up. Wrap in foil for a packed lunch.

chicken wraps

ingredients
serves 4

150 g/5½ oz natural yogurt
1 tbsp wholegrain mustard
280 g/10 oz cooked
    chicken breast, diced
140 g/5 oz iceberg lettuce,
    finely shredded
85 g/3 oz cucumber, thinly sliced
2 celery sticks, sliced
85 g/3 oz black seedless
    grapes, halved
4 flour tortillas
pepper

method

1 Combine the yogurt and mustard in a bowl and season
   to taste with pepper. Stir in the chicken and toss until
   thoroughly coated.

2 Put the lettuce, cucumber, celery and grapes into
   a separate bowl and mix well.

3 Fold a tortilla in half and in half again to make a cone
   that is easy to hold. Half-fill the tortilla pocket with
   the salad mixture and top with some of the chicken
   mixture. Repeat with the remaining tortillas, salad
   and chicken. Wrap in foil for a packed lunch.

turkey salad pitta

ingredients

serves 1

small handful baby leaf spinach,
    rinsed, patted dry and
    shredded
½ red pepper, deseeded
    and thinly sliced
½ carrot, peeled and coarsely
    grated
4 tbsp hummus
85 g/3 oz cooked turkey,
    thinly sliced
½ tbsp sunflower seeds
1 wholemeal pitta bread
salt and pepper

method

1 Put the spinach leaves, red pepper, carrot and hummus
   into a large bowl and stir together, so all the salad
   ingredients are coated with the hummus. Stir in the
   turkey and sunflower seeds and season to taste with
   salt and pepper.

2 Preheat the grill to high. Grill the pitta bread for about
   1 minute on each side to warm through, but do not
   brown. Cut it in half to make two 'pockets' of bread.

3 Divide the filling between the bread pockets. Wrap in
   foil for a packed lunch.

simply super sandwich fillings

ingredients
serves 4–8

crunchy tuna
200 g/7 oz canned tuna,
　drained and flaked
1 tbsp canned sweetcorn
　kernels, drained
1 tbsp chopped peppers
1 tbsp mayonnaise

fruity cheese spread
100 g/3½ oz low-fat soft cheese
1 tbsp chopped stoned dates
2 tbsp chopped ready-to-eat
　dried apricots

chicken & avocado
½ chicken breast, cooked
　and finely chopped
½ small avocado, mashed
　with 2 tsp lemon juice

scrambled egg & sausage
2 hard-boiled eggs, chopped
1 cooked sausage, chopped
1 tbsp mayonnaise

8 slices of wholemeal bread
butter, for spreading

method
1 Mix the ingredients for each filling together and
　store in an airtight container in the refrigerator
　until required.

2 Make up each sandwich between 2 slices of buttered
　bread and serve.

leek & potato soup

ingredients
serves 4–6

55 g/2 oz butter
1 onion, chopped
3 leeks, sliced
225 g/8 oz potatoes,
    peeled and cut into
    2-cm/³/₄-inch cubes
850 ml/1½ pints vegetable stock
150 ml/5 fl oz single cream
salt and pepper
fresh flat-leaf parsley sprigs,
    to garnish

method

1 Melt the butter in a large saucepan over a medium heat, add the onion, leeks and potatoes and sauté gently for 2–3 minutes, until soft but not brown. Pour in the stock, bring to the boil, then reduce the heat and simmer, covered, for 15 minutes.

2 Remove from the heat and liquidize the soup in the saucepan using a hand-held stick blender.

3 Heat the soup, season to taste with salt and pepper and transfer to serving bowls. Swirl with the cream, and garnish with parsley sprigs. Alternatively, transfer to a flask for a packed lunch.

chicken noodle soup

ingredients

serves 4

2 skinless, boneless chicken breasts
1.2 litres/2 pints chicken stock
3 carrots, peeled and cut into
    5-mm/¼-inch slices
85 g/3 oz vermicelli
    (or other fine noodles)
salt and pepper
1 tbsp fresh tarragon leaves

method

1 Place the chicken breasts in a large saucepan, add the
   stock and bring to a simmer. Cook for 25–30 minutes.
   Skim any scum from the surface if necessary. Remove
   the chicken from the water and keep warm.

2 Continue to simmer the stock, add the carrots and
   vermicelli and cook for 4–5 minutes.

3 Thinly slice or shred the chicken breasts and place
   in serving bowls.

4 Season the soup to taste with salt and pepper. Pour
   over the chicken and scatter with the tarragon leaves.
   Alternatively, stir the chicken and tarragon into the
   soup and transfer to a flask for a packed lunch.

spicy red lentil soup

ingredients

serves 4

300 g/10½ oz red lentils,
    picked over and rinsed
2 litres/3½ pints vegetable
    stock or water
2 green chillies, split
1 tsp turmeric
2 tbsp sunflower oil
1½ onions, thinly sliced
2 large garlic cloves, crushed
2 tsp curry paste, mild,
    medium or hot, to taste
salt and pepper
4 tbsp yogurt and chopped
    parsley, to garnish

method

1 Put the lentils and stock into a large saucepan with a tight-fitting lid. Place over a high heat and slowly bring to the boil, skimming the surface as necessary. Add the chillies and turmeric, reduce the heat to very low, cover the pan and leave the lentils to simmer for 25–30 minutes, until they are very soft and mushy.

2 Meanwhile, heat the oil in another large saucepan over a medium heat. Add the onions and garlic and fry for 5–7 minutes, until the onions are tender but not brown. Add the curry paste and cook, stirring, for about a minute. Add the lentil mixture to the pan, discarding the chillies.

3 Liquidize the soup in the saucepan using a hand-held stick blender. Add enough water to reach the desired consistency and slowly bring to the boil, then reduce the heat and simmer for 2 minutes. Season to taste with salt and pepper.

4 Ladle the soup into serving bowls, swirl in a little yogurt and sprinkle with parsley. Alternatively, transfer to a flask for a packed lunch.

spanish omelette

ingredients

serves 2

200 g/7 oz new potatoes
1 tbsp olive oil
1 onion, thinly sliced
1 red pepper, deseeded
    and thinly sliced
2 tomatoes, peeled, deseeded
    and chopped
6 large eggs
1 tbsp milk
2 tbsp finely grated
    Parmesan cheese
salt and pepper

method

1 Cook the potatoes in a saucepan of boiling water for
  8–12 minutes, until tender. Drain and leave to cool,
  then slice.

2 Heat the oil in an 18–20-cm/7–8-inch frying pan with
  a heatproof handle and cook the onion and red pepper
  until soft. Add the chopped tomatoes and cook for
  a further minute.

3 Add the potatoes to the pan and spread out evenly.

4 Beat the eggs, milk and cheese, with salt and pepper to
  taste, in a bowl and pour over the potato mixture. Cook
  for 4–5 minutes, until the eggs are set underneath.

5 Meanwhile, preheat the grill to high. Place the frying
  pan under the grill and cook the omelette for a further
  3–4 minutes, until the eggs are set.

6 Leave to cool, then cut into wedges and wrap in foil for
  a packed lunch.

variation

Replace the onions and red peppers with peas, beans,
carrots or mushrooms for an omelette that uses up
leftover vegetables.

cheesy sweetcorn fritters

ingredients

serves 2

1 egg
200 ml/7 fl oz milk
100 g/3½ oz plain flour
½ tsp baking powder
85 g/3 oz canned sweetcorn
    kernels, drained
4 tbsp grated Cheddar cheese
1 tsp snipped fresh chives
2 tsp sunflower oil
carrots and sweetcorn, to serve
    (optional)

method

1 Put the egg and milk into a small bowl and beat with a fork. Add the flour and baking powder and beat until smooth. Stir in the sweetcorn, cheese and chives.

2 Heat the oil in a frying pan and drop either teaspoonfuls or tablespoonfuls of the batter into it. Cook for 1–2 minutes on each side, until the fritters are puffed up and golden.

3 Drain on kitchen paper and serve immediately with cooked carrot batons and sweetcorn, if using. Alternatively, leave to cool and wrap in foil for a packed lunch.

bread, onion & tomato salad

ingredients

serves 2

2–3 bread rolls, depending on size
3 tbsp white wine vinegar
5 tbsp extra virgin olive oil
6 slices salami, chopped
1 tomato, chopped
1 large onion, halved and sliced
1 spring onion, finely chopped
salt and pepper

method

1 Break the bread rolls into pieces and place in a bowl. Pour over the vinegar and oil and leave to stand for 10 minutes, stirring frequently.

2 Add the salami, tomato and onion to the bread mixture. Season to taste with salt and pepper. Mix together carefully.

3 Scatter the spring onion over the salad before serving. Alternatively, transfer to an airtight container for a packed lunch.

roasted vegetable salad

ingredients

serves 4

1 onion
1 aubergine
1 red pepper, deseeded
1 orange pepper, deseeded
1 large courgette
2–4 garlic cloves
2–4 tbsp olive oil
1 tbsp balsamic vinegar
2 tbsp extra virgin olive oil
1 tbsp shredded fresh basil
salt and pepper
Parmesan cheese shavings,
    to serve

method

1 Preheat the oven to 200°C/400°F/Gas Mark 6.

2 Cut all the vegetables into even-sized wedges, put into
  a roasting tin and scatter over the garlic. Pour over
  2 tablespoons of the olive oil and toss the vegetables
  until well coated. Season to taste with salt and pepper.
  Roast in the preheated oven for 40 minutes, or until
  tender, adding the extra olive oil if needed.

3 Meanwhile, put the vinegar, extra virgin olive oil and
  salt and pepper to taste into a screw-top jar and shake
  until blended.

4 Once the vegetables are cooked, remove from the
  oven, arrange on a serving dish and pour over
  the dressing. Sprinkle with the basil and serve with
  Parmesan cheese shavings. Alternatively, leave to
  cool then transfer to an airtight container for a
  packed lunch.

rice salad

ingredients
serves 2

300 g/10½ oz cooked
   long-grain rice
1 red pepper, deseeded and
   chopped
1 leek, sliced
160 g/5¾ oz canned sweetcorn
   kernels, drained
5 basil leaves, sliced into strips
3 tbsp white wine vinegar
2 tbsp olive oil
salt and pepper

method

1 Place the cooked rice in a large bowl. Add the red pepper, leek and sweetcorn to the rice. Add the basil strips to the bowl.

2 Mix together the vinegar and oil in a small bowl, then season to taste with salt and pepper and pour over the rice salad.

3 Mix everything together well. Transfer to an airtight container for a packed lunch.

tabbouleh

ingredients

serves 4

175 g/6 oz bulgar wheat
3 tbsp extra virgin olive oil
4 tbsp lemon juice
4 spring onions, finely chopped
1 green pepper, deseeded
    and sliced
4 tomatoes, chopped
2 tbsp chopped fresh parsley
2 tbsp chopped fresh mint
8 black olives, stoned
salt and pepper

method

1 Place the bulgar wheat in a large bowl and add enough cold water to cover. Leave to stand for 30 minutes, or until doubled in size. Drain well and press out as much liquid as possible. Spread out the wheat on kitchen paper to dry.

2 Place the wheat in a serving bowl. Mix the oil and lemon juice together in a jug and season to taste with salt and pepper. Pour over the wheat and leave to marinate for 1 hour.

3 Add the spring onions, green pepper, tomatoes, parsley and mint to the salad and toss lightly to mix. Top the salad with the olives. Transfer to an airtight container for a packed lunch.

variation

Add a small amount of fresh chilli for extra spiciness. If you prefer a milder flavour, use a teaspoon of fresh ground cinnamon instead of the chillies.

barbecue chicken

ingredients

serves 4

4 chicken drumsticks, about
    100 g/3½ oz each, skinned
sliced spring onion, to garnish

barbecue sauce

1 shallot, finely chopped
1 garlic clove, crushed
1 tbsp tomato purée, blended
    with 150 ml/5 fl oz water
2 tbsp red wine vinegar
1 tbsp prepared mustard
1 tbsp Worcestershire sauce

method

1 To make the barbecue sauce, place the shallot, garlic, tomato purée mixture, vinegar, mustard and Worcestershire sauce in a screw-top jar, cover with the lid and shake vigorously until well blended.

2 Rinse the chicken drumsticks and pat dry with kitchen paper. Place the drumsticks in a large ovenproof dish, pour over the sauce and leave to stand for at least 2 hours, occasionally spooning the barbecue sauce over the chicken.

3 Preheat the oven to 190°C/375°F/Gas Mark 5. Cook the chicken drumsticks in the preheated oven for 20–25 minutes, or until the juices run clear when a skewer is inserted into the thickest part of the meat. Spoon the sauce over the chicken or turn the chicken over during cooking.

4 Serve immediately, sprinkled with spring onion. Alternatively, leave to cool and chill in the refrigerator until ready to serve.

mini savoury pies

ingredients

serves 6

butter, for greasing

200 g/7 oz ready-rolled puff pastry, thawed if frozen

plain flour, for dusting

3 eggs, beaten

125 ml/4 fl oz milk

85 g/3 oz mature Cheddar cheese, grated

1 slice ham, chopped (optional)

1 tomato, sliced

salt and pepper

method

1 Preheat the oven to 200°C/400°F/Gas Mark 6. Grease a deep 6-hole muffin tin.

2 Roll the pastry out on a lightly floured work surface until it is very thin. Cut out 6 rounds to fit the size of the muffin hole, making sure that the pastry extends just above the rim of the hole.

3 Whisk the eggs and milk together in a bowl and season to taste with salt and pepper. Divide the cheese between the pastry cases. Sprinkle with ham, if using, then pour the egg mixture over the top. Top each pie with a tomato slice.

4 Bake in the preheated oven for 20–25 minutes, or until risen and golden. Leave to cool slightly before removing the pies from the tin to serve.

cheese twists

ingredients

serves 4–6

butter, for greasing
85 g/3 oz Gruyère cheese, grated
½ tsp paprika
375 g/13 oz ready-rolled puff
    pastry, thawed if frozen
1 egg, beaten

method

1 Preheat the oven to 200°C/400°F/Gas Mark 6. Grease a large baking sheet.

2 Mix together the cheese and paprika and sprinkle over the sheet of puff pastry. Fold the puff pastry in half and roll out a little to seal the edges.

3 Cut the pastry into long 1-cm/½-inch wide strips, then cut each strip in half and gently twist. Place on the prepared baking sheet. Brush with the beaten egg and bake in the preheated oven for 10–12 minutes, or until crisp and golden. Place on a wire rack and leave to cool before serving.

banana loaf

ingredients

serves 8

butter, for greasing
125 g/4½ oz white
    self-raising flour
100 g/3½ oz self-raising flour
150 g/5½ oz demerara sugar
pinch of salt
½ tsp ground cinnamon
½ tsp ground nutmeg
2 large ripe bananas
175 ml/6 fl oz orange juice
2 eggs, beaten
4 tbsp sunflower oil

method

1 Preheat the oven to 180°C/350°F/Gas Mark 4. Lightly grease and line a 900-g/2-lb loaf tin.

2 Sift the flours, sugar, salt and the spices into a large bowl. In a separate bowl mash the bananas with the orange juice, then stir in the eggs and oil. Pour into the dry ingredients and mix well.

3 Spoon into the prepared tin and bake in the preheated oven for 1 hour. Test to see if the loaf is cooked by inserting a skewer into the centre. If it comes out clean, the loaf is done. If not, bake for a further 10 minutes and test again.

4 Remove from the oven and leave to cool in the tin. Turn out the loaf, slice and serve.

peanut butter cookies

ingredients

makes 28

115 g/4 oz butter, softened,
    plus extra for greasing
115 g/4 oz crunchy peanut butter
115 g/4 oz caster sugar
115 g/4 oz light muscovado sugar
1 egg, beaten
½ tsp vanilla extract
85 g/3 oz plain flour
½ tsp bicarbonate of soda
½ tsp baking powder
pinch of salt
115 g/4 oz rolled oats

method

1 Preheat the oven to 180°C/350°F/Gas Mark 4. Grease a large baking tray.

2 Place the butter and peanut butter in a bowl and beat together well. Beat in the caster sugar and muscovado sugar, then gradually beat in the egg and the vanilla extract.

3 Sift the flour, bicarbonate of soda, baking powder and salt into the mixture, add the rolled oats and stir until just combined.

4 Place spoonfuls of the mixture onto the prepared baking trays, spaced well apart to allow for spreading. Flatten slightly with a fork.

5 Bake in the preheated oven for 12 minutes, or until lightly browned. Leave the cookies to cool on the baking tray for 2 minutes, then transfer to a wire rack to cool completely before serving.

no-bake chocolate cake

ingredients

serves 6-8

225 g/8 oz plain chocolate,
   broken into pieces
225 g/8 oz unsalted butter
3 tbsp black coffee
55 g/2 oz light brown sugar
few drops of vanilla extract
225 g/8 oz digestive
   biscuits, crushed
85 g/3 oz raisins
85 g/3 oz walnuts, chopped

method

1 Line a 450-g/1-lb loaf tin with baking paper. Melt the chocolate, butter, coffee, sugar and vanilla extract in a saucepan over a low heat.

2 Stir in the crushed biscuits, raisins and walnuts and stir well. Spoon the mixture into the prepared loaf tin.

3 Leave to set for 1–2 hours in the refrigerator, then turn out and cut into thin slices to serve.

simple
suppers

baked chilli cheese sandwiches

ingredients

serves 4

350 g/12 oz Cheddar cheese, grated
150 g/5½ oz butter, softened, plus extra to finish
4 fresh green chillies, deseeded and chopped
½ tsp ground cumin
8 thick slices of bread

method

1 Preheat the oven to 190°C/375°F/Gas Mark 5.

2 Mix the cheese and 115 g/4 oz of the butter together in a bowl until combined, then add the chillies and cumin and stir in.

3 Use the extra butter to spread over one side of each slice of bread. Place 4 slices, butter-side down, on a baking sheet, then spread the cheese mixture over the top. Top with the remaining slices of bread, butter-side up and press down.

4 Bake in the preheated oven for 8–10 minutes, until crisp and lightly browned. Serve immediately.

mini muffin pizzas

ingredients

serves 6

3 wholemeal English muffins, halved
2 tbsp tomato purée
2 tbsp pesto
1 tbsp olive oil
1/2 red onion, thinly sliced
3 mushrooms, sliced
1/2 courgette, thinly sliced
2–3 slices ham or 6 slices salami
100 g/3 1/2 oz Cheddar cheese, grated, or 6 slices mozzarella cheese

method

1 Preheat the grill to high. Toast the muffins until golden, then leave to cool. Do not turn off the grill.

2 Mix the tomato purée and pesto together in a small bowl and spread equally over the muffin halves.

3 Heat the oil in a non-stick frying pan and then cook the onion, mushrooms and courgette until soft and beginning to brown.

4 Divide the vegetables between the muffins and top with the ham and then the cheese.

5 Cook under the preheated grill for 3–4 minutes, until the cheese is melted and browned. Serve hot or cold.

italian steak sandwiches

ingredients
serves 4

1 tbsp olive oil, plus extra for
  brushing
1 small onion, finely chopped
1 garlic clove, finely chopped
1 small red pepper, deseeded
  and finely chopped
100 g/3½ oz button mushrooms,
  finely chopped
200 g/7 oz fresh beef steak mince
125 ml/4 fl oz red wine
2 tbsp tomato purée
4 bread rolls
75 g/2¾ oz mozzarella cheese
2 tbsp torn fresh basil leaves
salt and pepper

method

1 Heat the oil in a large saucepan over a medium heat, add the onion, garlic, pepper and mushrooms and cook, stirring occasionally, for 5–10 minutes, until softened and beginning to brown.

2 Add the mince and cook, stirring frequently and breaking up any lumps with a wooden spoon, for 5 minutes, or until well browned. Add the wine, tomato purée and salt and pepper to taste and leave to simmer for 10 minutes, stirring occasionally. Remove from the heat.

3 Split the bread rolls in half and brush both halves with oil. Put the bottom halves onto a piece of foil and spoon an equal quantity of the sauce on top of each.

4 Slice the cheese, then divide between the bottoms of the rolls and arrange on top of the sauce. Add the basil leaves and cover with the tops of the rolls. Press down gently and wrap in the foil. Leave the sandwiches for at least 1 hour before serving.

mushroom fajitas

ingredients

serves 4-8

500 g/1 lb 2 oz large flat
    mushrooms
2 tbsp oil
1 onion, sliced
1 red pepper, deseeded
    and sliced
1 green pepper, deseeded
    and sliced
1 garlic clove, crushed
$1/4 - 1/2$ tsp cayenne pepper
grated rind and juice of 2 limes
2 tsp sugar
1 tsp dried oregano
8 flour tortillas
salt and pepper
lime wedges, to garnish

method

1 Cut the mushrooms into strips. Heat the oil in a large
  heavy-based frying pan. Add the mushrooms, onion,
  red and green peppers and garlic and stir-fry for 8–10
  minutes, until the vegetables are cooked.

2 Add the cayenne pepper, grated lime rind and juice,
  sugar and oregano. Season to taste with salt and
  pepper and cook for a further 2 minutes.

3 Meanwhile, heat the tortillas according to the packet
  instructions. Divide the mushroom mixture between
  the warmed tortillas and roll up. Serve immediately,
  garnished with lime wedges.

chorizo & cheese quesadillas

ingredients

serves 4–8

115 g/4 oz mozzarella cheese, grated
115 g/4 oz Cheddar cheese, grated
225 g/8 oz chorizo sausage (outer casing removed) or ham, diced
4 spring onions, finely chopped
2 fresh green chillies, deseeded and finely chopped
8 flour tortillas
vegetable oil, for brushing
salt and pepper

method

1 Place the cheeses, chorizo, spring onions, chillies and salt and pepper to taste in a bowl and mix together.

2 Divide the mixture between 4 of the flour tortillas, then top with the remaining tortillas.

3 Brush a large heavy-based frying pan with oil and heat over a medium heat. Add 1 quesadilla and cook, pressing it down with a spatula, for 4–5 minutes, until the underside is crisp and lightly browned. Turn over and cook the other side until the cheese has melted. Remove from the frying pan and keep warm. Cook the remaining quesadillas.

4 Cut each quesadilla into quarters, arrange on a warmed serving plate and serve.

yaki soba

ingredients

serves 2

400 g/14 oz ramen noodles
1 onion, finely sliced
200 g/7 oz beansprouts
1 red pepper, deseeded and finely
    shredded
about 150 g/5½ oz cooked
    chicken breast, sliced
12 cooked peeled prawns
1 tbsp oil
2 tbsp shoyu (Japanese soy sauce)
½ tbsp mirin
1 tsp sesame oil
1 tsp roasted sesame seeds
2 spring onions, finely sliced

method

1 Cook the noodles according to the packet instructions, drain well and tip into a bowl.

2 Mix the onion, beansprouts, red pepper, chicken and prawns together in a separate bowl. Stir through the noodles.

3 Preheat a wok over a high heat. Add the oil and heat until very hot. Add the noodle mixture and stir-fry for 4 minutes, or until golden, then add the shoyu, mirin and sesame oil and toss together.

4 Divide the mixture between 2 plates, sprinkle with the sesame seeds and spring onions and serve immediately.

spaghetti olio e aglio

ingredients

serves 4

450 g/1 lb dried spaghetti
125 ml/4 fl oz extra virgin olive oil
3 garlic cloves, finely chopped
3 tbsp chopped fresh
   flat-leaf parsley
salt and pepper

method

1 Bring a large saucepan of lightly salted water to the boil. Add the pasta, return to the boil and cook for 8–10 minutes, or until tender but still firm to the bite.

2 Meanwhile, heat the oil in a frying pan. Add the garlic and a pinch of salt and cook over a low heat, stirring constantly, for 3–4 minutes, or until golden. Do not allow the garlic to brown or it will taste bitter. Remove the frying pan from the heat.

3 Drain the pasta and transfer to a serving dish. Pour in the garlic-flavoured olive oil, then add the chopped parsley and season to taste with salt and pepper. Toss well and serve immediately.

spaghetti with tomatoes & basil

ingredients

serves 4

5 tbsp extra virgin olive oil
1 onion, finely chopped
800 g/1 lb 12 oz canned
    chopped tomatoes
4 garlic cloves, cut into quarters
450 g/1 lb dried spaghetti
large handful fresh basil leaves,
    shredded
salt and pepper
Parmesan cheese shavings,
    to serve

method

1 Heat the oil in a large saucepan over a medium heat.
   Add the onion and cook gently for 5 minutes, until soft.
   Add the tomatoes and garlic. Bring to the boil, then
   simmer over a low–medium heat for 25–30 minutes,
   or until the oil separates from the tomatoes. Season
   to taste with salt and pepper.

2 Bring a large saucepan of lightly salted water to the
   boil. Add the pasta, return to the boil and cook for
   8–10 minutes, or until tender but still firm to the bite.
   Drain and transfer to a serving dish.

3 Pour the sauce over the pasta. Add the basil and toss
   well to mix. Serve with the Parmesan cheese.

mushroom & spinach pasta

ingredients

serves 4

300 g/10½ oz dried penne
2 tbsp olive oil
250 g/9 oz mushrooms, sliced
1 tsp dried oregano
250 ml/9 fl oz vegetable stock
1 tbsp lemon juice
6 tbsp cream cheese
200 g/7 oz spinach leaves
salt and pepper

method

1 Bring a large saucepan of lightly salted water to the boil. Add the pasta, return to the boil and cook for 8–10 minutes, until tender but still firm to the bite. Drain, reserving 175 ml/6 fl oz of the cooking liquid.

2 Meanwhile, heat the oil in a large frying pan, add the mushrooms and cook, stirring frequently, for 8 minutes. Stir in the oregano, stock and lemon juice and cook for 10–12 minutes, or until reduced.

3 Stir in the cream cheese and spinach and cook over a low–medium heat for 3–5 minutes. Add the reserved cooking liquid, then the cooked pasta. Stir together well, season to taste with salt and pepper and heat through before serving.

spaghetti alla carbonara

ingredients

serves 4

450 g/1 lb dried spaghetti
1 tbsp olive oil
225 g/8 oz streaky bacon,
    chopped
4 eggs
5 tbsp single cream
2 tbsp freshly grated
    Parmesan cheese
salt and pepper

method

1 Bring a large saucepan of lightly salted water to the boil. Add the pasta, return to the boil and cook for 8–10 minutes, or until tender but still firm to the bite.

2 Meanwhile, heat the oil in a frying pan. Add the bacon and cook over a medium heat, stirring frequently, for 8–10 minutes.

3 Beat the eggs with the cream in a small bowl and season to taste with salt and pepper. Drain the pasta and return it to the saucepan. Tip in the contents of the frying pan, then add the egg mixture and half the Parmesan cheese. Stir well, then transfer to a serving dish. Serve immediately, sprinkled with the remaining cheese.

tuna-noodle casserole

ingredients

serves 4-6

200 g/7 oz dried tagliatelle
25 g/1 oz butter
55 g/2 oz fresh breadcrumbs
400 ml/14 fl oz canned
    condensed cream of
    mushroom soup
125 ml/4 fl oz milk
2 celery sticks, chopped
1 red and 1 green pepper,
    deseeded and chopped
140 g/5 oz mature Cheddar
    cheese, grated
2 tbsp chopped fresh parsley
200 g/7 oz canned tuna in oil,
    drained and flaked
salt and pepper

method

1 Preheat the oven to 200°C/400°F/Gas Mark 6.

2 Bring a large saucepan of lightly salted water to the boil. Add the pasta and cook for 2 minutes less than specified on the packet instructions. Meanwhile, melt the butter in a saucepan over a medium heat. Stir in the breadcrumbs, then remove from the heat and reserve.

3 Drain the pasta well and reserve. Pour the soup into the pasta pan over a medium heat, then stir in the milk, celery, peppers, half the cheese and all the parsley. Add the tuna and gently stir in so that the flakes don't break up. Season to taste with salt and pepper. Heat just until small bubbles appear around the edge of the mixture.

4 Stir the pasta into the pan and use 2 forks to mix all the ingredients together. Spoon the mixture into an ovenproof dish and spread out. Stir the remaining cheese into the breadcrumbs, then sprinkle over the top of the pasta mixture. Bake in the preheated oven for 20–25 minutes, until golden. Leave to stand for 5 minutes before serving straight from the dish.

variation

Replace the tuna with a couple of handfuls of chopped mushrooms for a vegetarian alternative.

macaroni cheese

ingredients

serves 4

600 ml/1 pint milk
1 onion, peeled
8 peppercorns
1 bay leaf
55 g/2 oz butter
40 g/1½ oz plain flour
½ tsp ground nutmeg
5 tbsp double cream
100 g/3½ oz mature Cheddar
    cheese, grated
100 g/3½ oz Roquefort cheese,
    crumbled
350 g/12 oz dried macaroni
100 g/3½ oz Gruyère or
    Emmenthal cheese, grated
pepper

method

1 Put the milk, onion, peppercorns and bay leaf in a pan and bring to the boil. Remove from the heat and leave to stand for 15 minutes.

2 Melt the butter in a pan and stir in the flour until well combined and smooth. Cook over a medium heat, stirring constantly, for 1 minute. Remove from the heat. Strain the milk to remove the solids and stir a little into the butter and flour mixture until well incorporated. Return the pan to the heat and gradually add the remaining milk, stirring constantly, until it has all been incorporated. Cook for a further 3 minutes, or until the sauce is smooth and thickened, then add the nutmeg, cream and pepper to taste. Add the Cheddar and Roquefort cheeses and stir until melted.

3 Meanwhile, bring a large saucepan of water to the boil. Add the macaroni, return to the boil and cook for 8–10 minutes, or until tender but still firm to the bite. Drain well and add to the cheese sauce. Stir together well.

4 Preheat the grill to high. Spoon the mixture into an ovenproof dish, scatter over the Gruyère cheese and grill until bubbling and brown. Serve immediately.

sausages & mash with onion gravy

ingredients

serves 4

8 pork sausages
1 tbsp oil

onion gravy

3 onions, cut in half and
    thinly sliced
70 g/2½ oz butter
250 ml/9 fl oz vegetable stock
salt and pepper

mashed potato

900 g/2 lb floury potatoes,
    such as King Edwards,
    Maris Piper or Desirée,
    peeled and cut into chunks
55 g/2 oz butter
3 tbsp hot milk
2 tbsp chopped fresh parsley
salt and pepper

method

1 Cook the sausages slowly in a frying pan with the oil over a low heat. Cover the pan and turn the sausages from time to time. Don't rush the cooking because you want them well-cooked and sticky. This will take 25–30 minutes.

2 Meanwhile, prepare the onion gravy by placing the onions in a frying pan with the butter and frying over a low heat until soft, stirring constantly. Continue to cook until they are brown and almost melting, stirring from time to time. This will take about 30 minutes, but it is worth it as the onions will naturally caramelize.

3 Pour in the stock and continue to bubble away until the onion gravy is really thick. Season to taste with salt and pepper.

4 To make the mashed potato, cook the potatoes in a large saucepan of boiling salted water for 15–20 minutes. Drain well and mash with a potato masher until smooth. Season to taste with salt and pepper, add the butter, milk and parsley and stir well.

5 Serve the sausages with the mashed potato and the onion gravy spooned over the top.

boston baked beans

ingredients

serves 2

4 chipolata sausages
400 g/14 oz canned white beans
   such as haricot, cannellini or
   butter, drained and rinsed
200 ml/7 fl oz passata
1 tbsp maple syrup
1 tsp wholegrain mustard
4 rashers streaky bacon

method

1 Preheat the grill to high. Grill the sausages, turning frequently, for about 10 minutes, or until browned and cooked through. Do not turn off the grill.

2 Put the beans, passata, maple syrup and mustard into a saucepan. Cook gently for about 10 minutes, until heated through.

3 Cook the bacon under the preheated grill until crisp and browned. Slice the sausages and add to the beans in the pan. Transfer to serving plates, top with the bacon, and serve immediately.

spicy fried eggs

ingredients
serves 2

2 tbsp olive oil
1 large onion, finely chopped
2 green or red peppers, deseeded
    and roughly chopped
1 garlic clove, finely chopped
½ tsp dried chilli flakes
4 plum tomatoes, peeled and
    roughly chopped
2 eggs
1 tbsp chopped fresh flat-leaf
    parsley
salt and pepper

method

1 Heat the oil in a large non-stick frying pan over a
    medium heat. Add the onion and cook until golden.
    Add the peppers, garlic and chilli flakes and cook until
    the peppers are soft.

2 Stir in the tomatoes, season to taste with salt and
    pepper and simmer over a low–medium heat for
    10 minutes.

3 Using the back of a spoon, make 2 depressions in
    the mixture in the frying pan. Break the eggs into the
    depressions, cover and cook for 3–4 minutes, until
    the eggs are set. Sprinkle with the parsley and serve.

pepper & mushroom hash

ingredients

serves 4

675 g/1 lb 8 oz potatoes, peeled
    and diced
1 tbsp olive oil
2 garlic cloves, crushed
1 green pepper, deseeded
    and diced
1 yellow pepper, deseeded
    and diced
3 tomatoes, diced
75 g/2¾ oz button mushrooms,
    halved
1 tbsp Worcestershire sauce
2 tbsp chopped fresh basil, plus
    extra sprigs to garnish
salt and pepper

method

1 Cook the potatoes in a large saucepan of lightly salted boiling water for 7–8 minutes. Drain well and reserve.

2 Heat the oil in a large frying pan. Add the potatoes and cook over a medium heat, stirring constantly, for about 8–10 minutes, until browned.

3 Add the garlic and peppers and cook, stirring frequently, for 2–3 minutes.

4 Stir in the tomatoes and mushrooms and cook, stirring frequently, for 5–6 minutes.

5 Stir in the Worcestershire sauce and basil and season to taste with salt and pepper. Transfer to a serving dish, garnish with basil sprigs, and serve immediately.

potato skins with tomato & sweetcorn salsa

ingredients

serves 2

2 large baking potatoes
oil, for brushing
55 g/2 oz Cheddar cheese, grated

salsa

85 g/3 oz canned sweetcorn
    kernels
55 g/2 oz canned kidney beans
2 tbsp olive oil
115 g/4 oz tomatoes, deseeded
    and diced
2 shallots, finely sliced
¼ red pepper, finely diced
1 fresh red chilli, deseeded and
    finely chopped
1 tbsp chopped fresh coriander
    leaves
1 tbsp lime juice
salt and pepper

method

1 Preheat the oven to 200°C/400°F/Gas Mark 6.

2 Prick the potatoes in several places with a fork and brush with oil. Cook directly on the oven shelf for 1 hour, or until the skins are crispy and the insides are soft when pierced with a fork.

3 Meanwhile, make the salsa. Drain the sweetcorn and beans, rinse well, then drain again. Put in a bowl with the oil, tomatoes, shallots, red pepper, chilli, coriander, lime juice and salt and pepper to taste and mix well together.

4 Preheat the grill to medium. Cut the potatoes in half lengthways. Scoop out the flesh (reserve for use in another recipe), leaving the skins intact. Brush the insides with oil, then put on a baking tray, cut-sides up. Grill for 5 minutes, or until crisp.

5 Spoon the salsa into the potato skins and sprinkle the cheese over the top. Return the filled potato skins to the preheated grill and cook gently until the cheese has melted. Serve immediately.

beyond the take-away

thai green chicken curry

ingredients

serves 4

2 tbsp groundnut or sunflower oil
2 tbsp Thai green curry paste
500 g/1 lb 2 oz skinless,
    boneless chicken breasts,
    cut into chunks
2 kaffir lime leaves, roughly torn
1 lemon grass stalk, finely chopped
225 ml/8 fl oz coconut milk
2 aubergines, cut into chunks
2 tbsp Thai fish sauce
fresh Thai basil sprigs and thinly
    sliced kaffir lime leaves,
    to garnish

method

1 Heat the oil in a preheated wok or large, heavy-based frying pan. Add the curry paste and stir-fry briefly until all the aromas are released.

2 Add the chicken, lime leaves and lemon grass and stir-fry for 3–4 minutes, until the meat is beginning to colour.

3 Add the coconut milk and aubergines and simmer gently for 8–10 minutes, or until tender.

4 Stir in the fish sauce and serve immediately, garnished with sprigs of Thai basil and lime leaves.

vegetable korma

ingredients

serves 4

4 tbsp ghee or vegetable oil
2 onions, chopped
2 garlic cloves, chopped
1 fresh red chilli, chopped
1 tbsp grated fresh ginger
2 tomatoes, peeled and chopped
1 orange pepper, deseeded
    and cut into small pieces
1 large potato, peeled and
    cut into chunks
200 g/7 oz cauliflower florets
1/2 tsp salt
1 tsp ground turmeric
1 tsp ground cumin
1 tsp ground coriander
1 tsp garam masala
200 ml/7 fl oz vegetable
    stock or water
150 ml/5 fl oz natural yogurt
150 ml/5 fl oz single cream
25 g/1 oz fresh coriander, chopped
freshly cooked rice, to serve

method

1 Heat the ghee in a large saucepan over a medium heat, add the onions and garlic and cook, stirring, for 3 minutes.

2 Add the chilli and ginger and cook for a further 4 minutes. Add the tomatoes, orange pepper, potato, cauliflower, salt and spices and cook, stirring, for a further 3 minutes.

3 Stir in the stock and bring to the boil. Reduce the heat and simmer for 25 minutes.

4 Stir in the yogurt and cream and cook gently, stirring, for a further 5 minutes. Add the fresh coriander and heat through. Serve with rice.

chicken chow mein

ingredients

serves 4

250 g/9 oz dried medium
    egg noodles
2 tbsp sunflower oil
250 g/9 oz cooked chicken
    breasts, shredded
1 garlic clove, finely chopped
1 red pepper, deseeded
    and thinly sliced
100 g/3½ oz chestnut
    mushrooms, sliced
6 spring onions, sliced
100 g/3½ oz fresh beansprouts
3 tbsp soy sauce
1 tbsp sesame oil

method

1 Cook the noodles according to the packet instructions.

2 Heat the sunflower oil in a large preheated wok. Add the chicken, garlic, red pepper, mushrooms, spring onions and beansprouts to the wok and stir-fry for about 5 minutes.

3 Drain the noodles thoroughly. Add the noodles to the wok, toss well and stir-fry for a further 5 minutes.

4 Drizzle the soy sauce and sesame oil over the chow mein and toss until well combined.

5 Transfer to serving bowls and serve immediately.

sesame hot noodles

ingredients

serves 6

500 g/1 lb 2 oz dried medium
    egg noodles
3 tbsp sunflower oil
2 tbsp sesame oil
1 garlic clove, crushed
1 tbsp smooth peanut butter
1 small green chilli, deseeded
    and very finely chopped
3 tbsp toasted sesame seeds
4 tbsp light soy sauce
½ tbsp lime juice
4 tbsp chopped fresh coriander
salt and pepper

method

1 Cook the noodles according to the packet instructions.

2 Meanwhile, make the dressing. Mix together the sunflower oil, sesame oil, garlic and peanut butter in a mixing bowl until smooth.

3 Add the chilli, sesame seeds and soy sauce to the bowl. Add the lime juice and mix well. Season to taste with salt and pepper.

4 Drain the noodles thoroughly, then place in a heated serving bowl.

5 Add the dressing and the chopped coriander to the noodles and toss well to mix. Serve immediately.

classic stir-fried vegetables

ingredients

serves 4

2 tbsp sesame oil

8 spring onions, finely chopped

1 garlic clove, crushed

1 tbsp grated fresh ginger

1 head of broccoli, cut into florets

1 orange or yellow pepper, deseeded and roughly chopped

125 g/4½ oz red cabbage, shredded

125 g/4½ oz baby corn

175 g/6 oz field mushrooms, thinly sliced

200 g/7 oz fresh beansprouts

250 g/9 oz canned water chestnuts, drained

4 tsp soy sauce, or to taste

method

1 Heat the oil in a large wok over a high heat. Stir-fry three quarters of the spring onions with the garlic and ginger for 30 seconds.

2 Add the broccoli, orange pepper and red cabbage and stir-fry for 1–2 minutes. Mix in the baby corn and mushrooms and stir-fry for a further 1–2 minutes.

3 Finally, add the beansprouts and water chestnuts and cook for a further 2 minutes. Pour in the soy sauce to taste and stir well.

4 Transfer to serving dishes and serve immediately, garnished with the remaining spring onions.

chicken skewers with satay sauce

ingredients

serves 4

4 skinless, boneless chicken
  breasts, about 140 g/5 oz each
2 tbsp olive oil
2 tbsp lemon juice

satay sauce

125 g/4½ oz smooth peanut
  butter
1½ tbsp olive oil
2 tbsp hot water
1½ tbsp light soy sauce
2 tbsp apple juice
4 tbsp coconut milk

method

1 To make the satay sauce, mix all the ingredients together in a bowl.

2 If you are using wooden skewers, soak them in cold water for at least 30 minutes to prevent them from burning. Cut each chicken breast lengthways into 4 strips and thread each strip onto a skewer.

3 Mix the oil and lemon juice together in a small bowl, then brush over the chicken.

4 Preheat the grill to medium–high. Grill for 3 minutes on each side until golden and cooked through, making sure that there is no trace of pink inside. Serve the skewers with the sauce.

shish kebabs

ingredients

serves 4–6

500 g/1 lb 2 oz boneless leg or
    neck of lamb with a small
    amount of fat, cut into
    2-cm/³/₄-inch cubes
2 green peppers, halved,
    deseeded and cut into
    2-cm/³/₄-inch pieces
1 onion, quartered and
    separated into layers
2 cherry tomatoes per skewer
tzatziki and lemon wedges,
    to serve

marinade

2 tbsp milk
2 tbsp olive oil, plus extra
    for brushing
1 large onion, grated
1 tbsp tomato purée
¹/₂ tsp ground cumin
salt and pepper

method

1 To make the marinade, put all the ingredients in a bowl and stir until combined. Add the lamb cubes and mix to coat well with the marinade. Cover and leave to marinate in the refrigerator for 2 hours.

2 Preheat the grill to high. If using wooden skewers presoak them for at least 30 minutes to prevent them from burning. Lightly brush the wooden or metal skewers with oil. Thread an equal quantity of the lamb cubes onto each, alternating with pieces of green pepper and onion, and the cherry tomatoes.

3 Brush the grill rack with oil. Add the kebabs and grill, turning frequently and basting with the remaining marinade, for 8–10 minutes, or until the lamb and peppers are charred on the edges.

4 Serve the kebabs with tzatziki and lemon wedges.

vegetable chilli

ingredients

serves 4

1 aubergine, cut into
    2.5-cm/1-inch slices
1 tbsp olive oil, plus extra
    for brushing
1 large red onion, finely chopped
2 red or yellow peppers,
    deseeded and finely chopped
3–4 garlic cloves,
    finely chopped or crushed
800 g/1 lb 12 oz canned
    chopped tomatoes
1 tbsp mild chilli powder
½ tsp ground cumin
½ tsp dried oregano
2 small courgettes, quartered
    lengthways and sliced
400 g/14 oz canned kidney beans,
    drained and rinsed
450 ml/16 fl oz water
1 tbsp tomato purée
6 spring onions, finely chopped
115 g/4 oz Cheddar cheese, grated
salt and pepper

method

1 Brush the aubergine slices on one side with oil. Heat half the oil in a large heavy-based frying pan over a medium–high heat. Add the aubergine slices, oiled-side up, and cook for 5–6 minutes, or until browned on one side. Turn over the slices, cook on the other side until browned and transfer to a plate. Cut into bite-sized pieces.

2 Heat the remaining oil in a large saucepan over a medium heat. Add the onion and peppers and cook, stirring occasionally, for 3–4 minutes, or until the onion is just softened but not browned.

3 Add the garlic and cook for a further 2–3 minutes, or until the onion is beginning to colour.

4 Add the tomatoes, chilli powder, cumin and oregano. Season to taste with salt and pepper. Bring to the boil, reduce the heat, cover and simmer for 15 minutes.

5 Add the courgettes, aubergine and kidney beans. Stir in the water and the tomato purée. Return to the boil, then cover and continue simmering for 45 minutes, or until the vegetables are tender. Ladle into bowls, top with the spring onions and cheese and serve.

chilli con carne

ingredients

serves 4

2 tbsp sunflower oil
500 g/1 lb 2 oz fresh beef mince
1 large onion, chopped
1 garlic clove, finely chopped
1 green pepper, deseeded
    and diced
1 tsp chilli powder
800 g/1 lb 12 oz canned
    chopped tomatoes
800 g/1 lb 12 oz canned
    red kidney beans,
    drained and rinsed
450 ml/16 fl oz beef stock
handful of fresh coriander sprigs,
    chopped, plus sprigs to garnish
salt and pepper
freshly cooked rice and soured
    cream, to serve

method

1 Heat the oil in a large heavy-based saucepan or flameproof casserole. Add the mince and cook over a medium heat, stirring frequently, for 5 minutes, or until broken up and browned.

2 Reduce the heat, then add the onion, garlic and green pepper to the pan and cook, stirring frequently, for 10 minutes.

3 Stir in the chilli powder, tomatoes and kidney beans. Pour in the stock and season to taste with salt. Bring to the boil, reduce the heat and simmer, stirring frequently, for about 15–20 minutes, or until the meat is tender.

4 Stir the chopped coriander into the meat. Transfer to serving bowls and garnish with the reserved coriander sprigs. Serve with rice and soured cream.

chicken fajitas with guacamole

ingredients

serves 4

1 tsp ground cumin
1 tbsp olive oil, plus extra
    for brushing
1 garlic clove, sliced
juice of 1 lime
4 skinless, boneless chicken
    breasts, about 115 g/4 oz
    each, cut into strips
4 flour tortillas
1 red pepper, deseeded and sliced
2 spring onions, diagonally sliced
salt and pepper

guacamole

1 large avocado,
    halved and stoned
1 garlic clove, crushed
juice of ½ lime
1 tbsp mayonnaise
salt and pepper

method

1 Mix the cumin, oil, garlic and lime juice together in a non-metallic shallow dish. Season the chicken to taste with salt and pepper, add to the dish and turn to coat in the marinade. Cover with clingfilm and leave to marinate in the refrigerator for up to 1 hour, turning the chicken occasionally.

2 To make the guacamole, scoop the flesh from the avocado halves into a bowl and mash together with the garlic and lime juice. Add the mayonnaise and salt and pepper to taste and mix until smooth and creamy. Set aside.

3 Preheat a griddle pan. Remove the chicken from the marinade, brush with oil and cook for 6–8 minutes, turning halfway through the cooking time, until cooked through and golden.

4 Meanwhile, warm the tortillas according to the packet instructions. Arrange an equal quantity of the chicken, red pepper and spring onions down the centre of each. Add a spoonful of guacamole and roll up. Slice diagonally in half to serve.

beef burgers with cheese

ingredients

serves 4

750 g/1 lb 10 oz fresh beef mince
1 beef stock cube
1 tbsp minced dried onion
2 tbsp water
55 g/2 oz grated Cheddar cheese
4 burger buns, split
tomato slices and lettuce leaves,
    to serve
chips, to serve (optional)

method

1 Place the mince in a large mixing bowl. Crumble the stock cube over the meat, add the dried onion and water and mix well. Divide the meat into 4 portions, shape each into a ball, then flatten slightly to make a burger shape of your preferred thickness.

2 Preheat a griddle pan over a high heat. Cook the burgers for about 5 minutes on each side, depending on how well done you like your meat and the thickness of the burgers. Press down occasionally with a spatula or palette knife during cooking.

3 Sprinkle the cheese on top of the burgers after you have turned them.

4 Place the burgers in buns on lettuce leaves, topped with tomato slices on the melted cheese. Serve immediately with chips, if using.

bean burgers

ingredients

serves 6

400 g/14 oz canned cannellini
    beans, drained and rinsed
2 tbsp red pesto
75 g/2¾ oz fresh wholemeal
    breadcrumbs
1 egg
2 tbsp olive oil
½ small red onion,
    finely chopped
1 garlic clove, crushed
6 granary rolls
6 tsp hummus
salt and pepper
cucumber slices, tomato slices
    and lettuce leaves, to serve

method

1 Mash the beans with a potato masher in a bowl until they are smooth, then add the pesto, breadcrumbs, egg and salt and pepper to taste, and mix well.

2 Heat half the oil in a non-stick frying pan over a low heat and cook the onion and garlic until soft. Add to the bean mixture and mix well.

3 Heat the remaining oil in the frying pan. Spoon in the bean mixture, in 6 separate mounds, then press each one down with the back of a spoon to form a burger.

4 Cook the burgers for 4–5 minutes, then carefully turn over and cook for a further 4–5 minutes, until golden.

5 Meanwhile, slice the rolls in half and spread the bottom half of each roll with a teaspoon of the hummus.

6 Remove the burgers from the frying pan and drain on kitchen paper. Place each one in a roll, and top with the cucumber slices, tomato slices and lettuce leaves. Serve immediately.

pizza

ingredients

serves 4

pizza base

225 g/8 oz strong white flour, plus extra for dusting
1 tsp easy-blend dried yeast
1 tsp salt
2 tbsp olive oil
225–350 ml/8–12 fl oz warm water

topping

4 tbsp olive oil
1 large onion, thinly sliced
6 button mushrooms, thinly sliced
½ small green pepper, ½ small red pepper and ½ small yellow pepper, deseeded and thinly sliced
300 g/10½ oz ready-made tomato pasta sauce
55 g/2 oz mozzarella cheese, thickly sliced
2 tbsp freshly grated Parmesan cheese
1 tsp chopped fresh basil

method

1 Combine the flour, yeast and salt in a mixing bowl. Drizzle over half the oil. Make a well in the centre and pour in the water. Mix to a firm dough and shape into a ball. Turn out onto a floured work surface and knead until it is smooth and elastic. Brush the bowl with the remaining oil. Put the dough in the bowl and turn to coat with oil. Cover with a clean tea towel and leave to rise for 1 hour.

2 When the dough has doubled in size, punch it down to release the excess air, then knead until smooth. Divide in half and roll into 2 thin rounds. Place on a baking sheet.

3 Preheat the oven to 220°C/425°F/Gas Mark 7.

4 For the topping, heat the oil in a frying pan and cook the onion, mushrooms and peppers for 5 minutes, or until softened. Spread some of the tomato sauce over the pizza bases, but do not go right to the edge. Top with the vegetables and mozzarella cheese. Spoon over more tomato sauce, then sprinkle with Parmesan cheese and basil. Bake in the preheated oven for 10–15 minutes, or until the base is crispy and the cheese has melted.

fish cakes

ingredients

serves 4

450 g/1 lb potatoes, peeled
450 g/1 lb mixed fish fillets,
    such as cod, haddock and
    salmon, skinned
2 tbsp chopped fresh parsley
    or tarragon
grated rind of 1 lemon
1 tbsp plain flour
1 egg, beaten
115 g/4 oz white or wholemeal
    breadcrumbs, made from
    day-old bread
4 tbsp vegetable oil
salt and pepper

method

1 Cut the potatoes into chunks and cook in a large saucepan of boiling salted water for 15 minutes. Drain well and mash with a potato masher until smooth.

2 Place the fish in a frying pan and just cover with water. Bring to the boil over a medium heat, then cover and simmer gently for 5 minutes, until just cooked. Remove from the heat and drain the fish onto a plate. When cool enough to handle, flake the fish and ensure that no bones remain.

3 Mix the potatoes with the fish, parsley and lemon rind in a bowl. Season well with salt and pepper and shape into 4 round, flat cakes.

4 Dust the fish cakes with flour, dip them into the beaten egg, then coat thoroughly in the breadcrumbs. Place on a baking sheet, cover with clingfilm and chill in the refrigerator for at least 30 minutes.

5 Heat the oil in the frying pan and fry the fish cakes over a medium heat for 5 minutes on each side. Use a palette knife or fish slice to turn them carefully. Serve.

chicken nuggets

ingredients

serves 4

4 tbsp dry breadcrumbs
2 tbsp finely grated Parmesan
    cheese
1 tsp dried thyme
1 tsp salt
pinch of pepper
2 skinless, boneless chicken
    breasts, cut into cubes
115 g/4 oz melted butter
barbecue sauce or tomato ketchup,
    to serve

method

1 Preheat the oven to 200°C/400°F/Gas Mark 6.

2 Combine the breadcrumbs, cheese, thyme, salt and pepper on a large plate or in a polythene bag.

3 Toss the chicken cubes in the melted butter, then in the crumb mixture. Place on a baking sheet and bake in the preheated oven for 10 minutes, until crisp.

4 Remove the chicken nuggets from the oven and serve with barbecue sauce or tomato ketchup.

falafel

ingredients

serves 4

225 g/8 oz dried chickpeas
1 large onion, finely chopped
1 garlic clove, crushed
2 tbsp chopped fresh parsley
2 tsp ground cumin
2 tsp ground coriander
¼ tsp baking powder
oil, for deep-frying
salt and cayenne pepper
hummus, tomato wedges and
    parsley sprigs, to serve

method

1 Soak the chickpeas overnight in enough cold water to cover them and allow room for expansion. Drain, then place in a saucepan, cover with fresh water and bring to the boil. Reduce the heat and simmer for 1 hour, or until tender. Drain.

2 Place the chickpeas in a food processor and blend to make a coarse paste. Add the onion, garlic, parsley, cumin, coriander, baking powder, and salt and cayenne pepper to taste. Blend again to mix thoroughly. Alternatively, mash the chickpeas in a bowl with a potato masher, then stir in the remaining ingredients.

3 Cover and leave to rest for 30 minutes, then shape into balls. Leave to rest for a further 30 minutes. Heat the oil in a deep-fat fryer or large saucepan to 180–190°C/350–375°F, or until a cube of bread browns in 30 seconds. Carefully drop in the balls and cook until golden brown. Remove from the oil and drain on kitchen paper.

4 Garnish with parsley sprigs and serve hot or at room temperature with hummus and tomato wedges.

hummus

ingredients

serves 6

400 g/14 oz canned chickpeas, drained
150 ml/5 fl oz tahini, well stirred
150 ml/5 fl oz water, plus extra for thinning
150 ml/5 fl oz olive oil, plus extra for drizzling
2 garlic cloves, roughly chopped
6 tbsp lemon juice
1 tbsp chopped fresh mint
salt and pepper
paprika, to serve

method

1 Put the chickpeas, tahini, oil and water into a tall beaker and process briefly using a hand-held stick blender. Add the garlic, lemon juice and mint and process until smooth.

2 Check the consistency of the hummus and, if it is too thick, add 1 tablespoon of water and process again. Continue adding water, 1 tablespoon at a time, until the right consistency is achieved. Hummus should have a thick, coating consistency. Season to taste with salt and pepper.

3 Spoon the hummus into a serving dish and drizzle with a little oil. Cover with clingfilm and chill in the refrigerator until required. To serve, dust lightly with paprika.

variation

For a Mexican hummus add chopped fresh coriander leaves and 2 jalapeño chillies, deseeded and finely chopped. Replace the lemon juice with lime juice and stir together.

pitta crisps

ingredients
makes 16

2 wholemeal pitta breads
olive oil, for brushing

method

1 Preheat the oven to 180°C/350°F/Gas Mark 4.

2 Using a serrated knife, split each pitta bread in half, then quarter each half to make a total of 16 pieces.

3 Place the pieces of pitta bread on a baking sheet, rough side up. Lightly brush each piece with oil, then bake in the preheated oven for 20 minutes, or until crisp and golden brown.

4 Leave to cool completely before serving with dips. These crisps will keep fresh in an airtight container for up to 3 days.

paprika crisps

ingredients

serves 4

2 large potatoes, peeled
3 tbsp olive oil
½ tsp paprika
salt

method

1 Slice the potatoes very thinly so that they are almost transparent and place in a bowl of cold water, then drain them thoroughly and pat dry with kitchen paper.

2 Heat the oil in a large heavy-based frying pan and add the paprika. Cook, stirring constantly, to ensure that the paprika doesn't catch on the base and burn.

3 Add the potato slices to the frying pan and cook them in a single layer over a low–medium heat for about 5 minutes, or until the potato slices are just beginning to curl slightly at the edges.

4 Carefully remove the potato slices from the pan using a slotted spoon and transfer them to kitchen paper to drain thoroughly.

5 Preheat the grill to medium. Sprinkle the potato slices with salt and grill, turning frequently, for 10 minutes, until they begin to go crisp. Sprinkle the crisps with a little more salt and serve immediately.

iced raspberry sundae

ingredients

serves 4

450 g/1 lb fresh raspberries,
plus extra to decorate
450 ml/16 fl oz double cream
55 g/2 oz flaked almonds
225 g/8 oz fresh or canned
cherries, stoned
15 g/½ oz plain chocolate, grated
fresh mint sprigs, to decorate

method

1 Preheat the oven to 200°C/400°F/Gas Mark 6.

2 Reserve 115 g/4 oz of the raspberries on one side
and lightly crush the remainder.

3 Whip the cream in a medium bowl until soft peaks
form. Put 4 tablespoons of the cream into a small bowl,
cover and reserve. Stir the crushed raspberries into the
remaining cream, spoon into a freezerproof container
and freeze for 1 hour, or until partially frozen.

4 Meanwhile, spread the almonds out on a baking sheet
and toast in the preheated oven, turning occasionally,
for 8–10 minutes, or until golden brown. Remove from
the oven and leave to cool.

5 Arrange the reserved raspberries and cherries in the
bases of 4 sundae glasses, then sprinkle with a few
toasted almonds. Cover with scoops of the frozen
raspberry mixture, then swirl the reserved cream on top.
Sprinkle with the grated chocolate and decorate with
extra raspberries and mint sprigs. Serve immediately.

chocolate ice-cream bites

ingredients

serves 6

600 ml/1 pint ice cream
200 g/7 oz plain chocolate,
    broken into pieces
2 tbsp unsalted butter

method

1 Line a baking tray with clingfilm. Using a melon baller, scoop out balls of ice cream and place them in paper cases on a baking tray. Alternatively, cut the ice cream into bite-sized cubes. Stick a cocktail stick in each piece and return to the freezer until very hard.

2 Place the chocolate and the butter in a heatproof bowl set over a saucepan of gently simmering water until melted. Quickly dip the frozen ice-cream balls into the warm chocolate and return to the freezer. Keep them there until ready to serve.

fruit skewers

ingredients

serves 2

a selection of fruit,
    such as apricots, peaches,
    figs, strawberries, mangoes,
    pineapple, bananas, dates
    and papaya, prepared and
    cut into chunks
2 tbsp maple syrup
50 g/1¼oz plain chocolate,
    broken into pieces

method

1 Soak 4 wooden skewers in water for at least 30 minutes to prevent them from burning. Thread alternate pieces of fruit onto each skewer. Brush the fruit with a little maple syrup.

2 Put the chocolate in a heatproof bowl set over a saucepan of gently simmering water, ensuring that the bowl does not touch the water, and heat until the chocolate has melted.

3 Preheat the grill to high and line the grill pan with foil. Grill the fruit skewers until caramelized. Serve drizzled with the melted chocolate.

look who's cooking

spaghetti bolognese

ingredients

serves 4

2 tbsp olive oil
1 onion, finely chopped
2 garlic cloves, finely chopped
1 carrot, peeled and finely chopped
85 g/3 oz mushrooms, sliced
1 tsp dried oregano
½ tsp dried thyme
1 bay leaf
280 g/10 oz fresh beef mince
300 ml/10 fl oz beef stock
300 ml/10 fl oz passata
350 g/12 oz dried spaghetti
salt and pepper

method

1 To make the sauce, heat the oil in a heavy-based, non-stick saucepan. Add the onion and sauté, half covered, for 5 minutes, or until softened. Add the garlic, carrot and mushrooms and sauté the mixture for a further 3 minutes, stirring occasionally.

2 Add the herbs and mince to the pan and cook until the meat has browned, stirring regularly.

3 Add the stock and passata. Reduce the heat, season to taste with salt and pepper and cook over a low–medium heat, half covered, for 15–20 minutes, or until the sauce has reduced and thickened. Remove the bay leaf.

4 Meanwhile, bring a large saucepan of lightly salted water to the boil. Add the pasta, return to the boil and cook for 8–10 minutes, until tender but still firm to the bite.

5 Drain the pasta, then mix together the pasta and sauce. Serve immediately.

spaghetti with meatballs

ingredients

serves 4

40 g/1½ oz fresh breadcrumbs
400 g/14 oz fresh beef mince
2 garlic cloves, crushed
1 large egg, lightly beaten
40 g/1½ oz Parmesan cheese,
    finely grated
flour, for coating
2 tbsp olive oil
2 garlic cloves, crushed
2 tsp dried oregano
800 g/1 lb 12 oz canned
    chopped tomatoes
1 tbsp tomato purée
1 tsp sugar
300 g/10½ oz dried spaghetti
salt and pepper

method

1 Place the breadcrumbs in a bowl with the beef, garlic, egg, cheese and salt and pepper to taste.

2 Mix the beef mixture until it comes together in a ball. Flour your hands and roll the mixture into walnut-sized balls. Chill the meatballs in the refrigerator while you make the sauce.

3 Heat the oil in a saucepan and add the garlic and oregano. Stir for 1 minute. Add the tomatoes, tomato purée and sugar. Bring to the boil, then reduce the heat and simmer for 8 minutes.

4 Carefully place the meatballs in the pan and spoon the sauce over them. Cover and simmer for 20 minutes, turning the meatballs occasionally.

5 Meanwhile, bring a large saucepan of lightly salted water to the boil. Add the pasta, return to the boil and cook for 8–10 minutes, until tender but still firm to the bite. Drain and serve with the meatballs and tomato sauce.

beef bourguignon

ingredients

serves 6

2 tbsp olive oil

175 g/6 oz unsmoked bacon,
   sliced into thin strips

1.3 kg/3 lb braising beef, cut into
   5-cm/2-inch pieces

2 carrots, peeled and sliced

2 onions, chopped

2 garlic cloves, very finely chopped

3 tbsp plain flour

700 ml/1¼ pints red wine

350–450 ml/12–16 fl oz
   beef stock

1 sachet bouquet garni

1 tsp salt

¼ tsp pepper

3 tbsp butter

350 g/12 oz shallots

350 g/12 oz button mushrooms

method

1 Heat the oil in a large flameproof casserole over a
   medium heat. Add the bacon and brown for 2–3
   minutes. Remove with a slotted spoon. Add the beef
   in batches and cook until browned. Drain and set aside
   with the bacon.

2 Add the carrots and chopped onions to the casserole
   and cook for 5 minutes. Add the garlic and fry until just
   coloured. Return the meat and bacon to the casserole.
   Sprinkle over the flour and cook for 1 minute, stirring.
   Add the wine, enough stock to cover, the bouquet
   garni, salt and pepper. Bring to the boil, cover and
   simmer gently for 3 hours.

3 Heat half the butter in a frying pan. Add the shallots,
   cover and cook until softened. Remove with a slotted
   spoon and keep warm. Heat the remaining butter in
   the frying pan. Add the mushrooms and fry briefly.
   Remove and keep warm.

4 Strain the casserole liquid through a sieve into a clean
   saucepan. Wipe out the casserole with kitchen paper
   and tip the meat mixture, mushrooms and shallots
   back in. Remove the surface fat from the cooking
   liquid, simmer for 1–2 minutes to reduce, then pour
   over the meat and vegetables. Serve.

beef goulash

ingredients

serves 4

2 tbsp vegetable oil
1 large onion, chopped
1 garlic clove, crushed
750 g/1 lb 10 oz lean
    braising beef
2 tbsp paprika
400 g/14 oz canned chopped
    tomatoes
2 tbsp tomato purée
1 large red pepper, deseeded
    and chopped
175 g/6 oz button mushrooms,
    sliced
600 ml/1 pint beef stock
1 tbsp cornflour
1 tbsp water
salt and pepper
fresh chopped parsley, to garnish
freshly cooked long-grain
    and wild rice, to serve

method

1 Heat the vegetable oil in a large heavy-based frying pan. Add the onion and garlic and cook over a low heat for 3–4 minutes.

2 Using a sharp knife, cut the beef into chunks, add to the frying pan and cook over a high heat for 3 minutes, or until browned. Add the paprika and stir well, then add the tomatoes, tomato purée, red pepper and mushrooms. Cook for a further 2 minutes, stirring frequently. Pour in the stock. Bring to the boil, reduce the heat, cover and simmer for 1½–2 hours, or until the meat is tender.

3 Blend the cornflour and water together in a small bowl, then add to the frying pan, stirring, until thickened and smooth. Cook for 1 minute. Season to taste with salt and pepper.

4 Transfer the beef goulash to a serving dish, garnish with parsley and serve with a mix of long-grain and wild rice.

roast chicken

ingredients

serves 6

1 chicken, weighing 2.25 kg/5 lb
55 g/2 oz butter
2 tbsp chopped fresh lemon
    thyme, plus extra to garnish
1 lemon, quartered, plus extra
    to garnish
125 ml/4 fl oz white wine
salt and pepper
roast potatoes, to serve

method

1 Preheat the oven to 220°C/425°F/Gas Mark 7. Make sure the chicken is clean, wiping it inside and out using kitchen paper, and place in a roasting tin.

2 Place the butter in a bowl and mash with a fork, then mix in the thyme and season well with salt and pepper. Butter the chicken all over with the herb butter, inside and out, and place the lemon quarters inside the body cavity. Pour the wine over the chicken.

3 Roast the chicken in the centre of the preheated oven for 20 minutes. Reduce the temperature to 190°C/375°F/Gas Mark 5 and continue to roast for a further 1¼ hours, basting frequently. Cover with foil if the skin begins to brown too much. If the tin dries out, add a little more wine or water.

4 Test that the chicken is cooked by piercing the thickest part of the leg with a sharp knife or skewer and making sure the juices run clear. Remove from the oven.

5 Remove the chicken from the roasting tin and place on a warmed serving plate to rest, covered with foil, for 10 minutes before carving. Serve with roast potatoes, garnished with pieces of lemon and lemon thyme.

southern fried chicken

ingredients

serves 4-6

1 chicken, weighing 1.5 kg/
    3 lb 5 oz, cut into 6–8 pieces
75 g/2¾ oz plain flour
2–4 tbsp butter
corn or groundnut oil,
    for shallow-frying
salt and pepper

method

1 Put the chicken into a large bowl with 1 teaspoon of salt and enough water to cover, then cover and chill in the refrigerator for at least 4 hours, but ideally overnight. Drain well and pat dry with kitchen paper.

2 Put the flour and salt and pepper to taste into a polythene bag. Add the chicken pieces and shake until well coated. Remove the chicken pieces from the bag and shake off any excess flour.

3 Melt 2 tablespoons of the butter with about 1 cm/ ½ inch of oil in a flameproof casserole or large frying pan with a lid over a medium–high heat. Do not leave unattended.

4 Add as many chicken pieces as will fit in a single layer without overcrowding, skin-side down. Cook for 5 minutes, or until the skin is golden and crisp. Turn the chicken over and cook for a further 10–15 minutes, covered, until the juices run clear when a skewer is inserted into the thickest part of the meat. Remove the chicken from the casserole and drain well on kitchen paper. Transfer to a low oven to keep warm while cooking any remaining pieces if serving hot, adding more butter and oil if necessary.

paella

ingredients

serves 2–3

2 tbsp olive oil
1 onion, diced
2 skinless, boneless chicken
    breasts, sliced
1 small red pepper, deseeded
    and diced
2 garlic cloves, chopped
1 tomato, deseeded and chopped
1 tbsp tomato purée
½ tsp ground turmeric
600 ml/1 pint chicken stock or
    vegetable stock
175 g/6 oz paella rice
55 g/2 oz frozen peas
115 g/4 oz cooked prawns,
    thawed if frozen
salt and pepper

method

1 Heat the oil in a large heavy-based frying pan with a lid. Add the onion and fry for 5 minutes, or until soft. Add the chicken, red pepper and garlic and sauté for 5 minutes over a medium heat, stirring frequently to prevent the mixture from sticking to the base of the pan.

2 Add the tomato, tomato purée, turmeric and stock to the pan. Stir in the rice and bring to the boil, then reduce the heat and simmer, covered, for 15 minutes, or until the rice is tender.

3 Add the peas, prawns and salt and pepper to taste and cook for a further 2–3 minutes, or until the prawns have heated through. Serve immediately.

roast vegetable lasagne

ingredients

serves 4

3 tbsp olive oil
4 courgettes, thickly sliced
3 red peppers, deseeded
    and chopped
1 aubergine, chopped
2 red onions, chopped
5 shallots, peeled and quartered
250 g/9 oz button mushrooms
400 g/14 oz canned chopped
    tomatoes
1 tbsp tomato purée
200 g/7 oz lasagne sheets
2 tbsp grated Parmesan cheese
salt and pepper

cheese sauce

50 g/1¾ oz butter
50 g/1¾ oz plain flour
600 ml/1 pint full-fat milk
100 g/3½ oz Cheddar cheese,
    grated

method

1 Preheat the oven to 190°C/375°F/Gas Mark 5.

2 Put the oil in a large bowl, add the courgettes, peppers, aubergine, onions and shallots and toss well to coat.

3 Divide the vegetables between 2 baking trays and roast in the preheated oven for 30–40 minutes, until soft and flecked with brown. Add the button mushrooms after 20 minutes.

4 Remove the vegetables from the oven and tip into a large bowl. Add the tomatoes and tomato purée and mix well.

5 To make the sauce, melt the butter in a saucepan over a low heat. Stir in the flour and cook, stirring constantly, for 2–3 minutes. Gradually add the milk and cook, continuing to stir constantly, until the sauce is thick and smooth. Season to taste with salt and pepper and stir in the Cheddar cheese.

6 Layer the vegetable mixture and sauce in an ovenproof dish with the lasagne sheets, finishing with a layer of sauce. Sprinkle over the Parmesan cheese and bake in the preheated oven for 30–35 minutes. Remove from the oven and serve immediately.

risotto

ingredients

serves 4

2 litres/3½ pints stock or water
1 tbsp olive oil
3 tbsp butter
1 small onion, finely chopped
450 g/1 lb risotto rice
55 g/2 oz Parmesan cheese,
    finely grated, plus extra
    shavings to garnish
salt and pepper

method

1 Bring the stock to the boil in a large saucepan, then reduce the heat and keep simmering gently over a low heat while you are cooking the risotto. Heat the oil with 2 tablespoons of the butter in a deep saucepan over a medium heat until the butter has melted. Stir in the onion and cook gently until soft.

2 Add the rice and mix to coat in the oil and butter. Cook and stir for 2–3 minutes, or until the grains are translucent. Gradually add the stock, a ladleful at a time. Stir constantly and add more liquid as the rice absorbs it. Increase the heat to medium so that the liquid bubbles. Cook for 20 minutes, or until all the liquid is absorbed. The risotto should be of a creamy consistency with a bit of bite in the rice.

3 Remove the risotto from the heat and add the remaining butter. Mix well, then stir in the grated Parmesan cheese and season to taste with salt and pepper. Serve topped with Parmesan cheese shavings.

stuffed red peppers with basil

ingredients

serves 4

140 g/5 oz long-grain white or
    brown rice
4 large red peppers
2 tbsp olive oil
1 garlic clove, chopped
4 shallots, chopped
1 celery stick, chopped
3 tbsp chopped toasted walnuts
2 tomatoes, peeled and chopped
1 tbsp lemon juice
50 g/1¾ oz raisins
4 tbsp freshly grated
    Cheddar cheese
2 tbsp chopped fresh basil
salt and pepper

method

1 Preheat the oven to 180°C/350°F/Gas Mark 4.

2 Cook the rice in a saucepan of lightly salted boiling water for 20 minutes if using white rice, or 35 minutes if using brown. Drain, rinse under cold running water, then drain again.

3 Using a sharp knife, cut the tops off the peppers and reserve. Remove the seeds and white cores, then blanch the peppers and reserved tops in boiling water for 2 minutes. Remove from the heat and drain well. Set aside.

4 Heat half the oil in a large frying pan. Add the garlic and shallots and cook, stirring, for 3 minutes. Add the celery, walnuts, tomatoes, lemon juice and raisins and cook for a further 5 minutes. Remove from the heat and stir in the rice, cheese and basil and season to taste with salt and pepper.

5 Stuff the peppers with the rice mixture and arrange them in a baking dish. Place the tops on the peppers, drizzle over the remaining oil, loosely cover with foil and bake in the preheated oven for 45 minutes. Serve immediately.

perfect roast potatoes

ingredients

serves 6

1.3 kg/3 lb large floury potatoes, peeled and cut into even-sized chunks
3 tbsp olive oil
salt

method

1 Preheat the oven to 220°C/425°F/Gas Mark 7.

2 Cook the potatoes in a large saucepan of lightly salted boiling water over a medium heat, covered, for 5–7 minutes. They will still be firm. Remove from the heat. Meanwhile, add the fat to a roasting tin and place in the preheated oven.

3 Drain the potatoes well and return them to the saucepan. Cover and firmly shake the pan so that the surface of the potatoes is slightly roughened.

4 Remove the roasting tin from the oven and carefully tip the potatoes into the hot oil. Baste them to ensure that they are all coated with it.

5 Roast the potatoes at the top of the oven for 45–50 minutes, turning once, until they are browned all over. Using a slotted spoon, carefully transfer the potatoes to a serving dish and sprinkle with salt before serving.

garlic mash

ingredients

serves 4

900 g/2 lb floury potatoes,
   peeled and cut into chunks
8 garlic cloves, crushed
150 ml/5 fl oz milk
85 g/3 oz butter
pinch of ground nutmeg
salt and pepper
1 tbsp chopped fresh flat-leaf
   parsley, to garnish

method

1 Put the potatoes in a large saucepan. Add enough cold water to cover and a pinch of salt. Bring to the boil and cook for 10 minutes. Add the garlic and cook for a further 10 minutes, until the potatoes are tender.

2 Drain the potatoes and garlic thoroughly, reserving 3 tablespoons of the cooking liquid.

3 Return the reserved liquid to the pan, add the milk and bring to simmering point. Add the butter and return the potatoes and garlic to the pan. Mash thoroughly with a potato masher.

4 Season to taste with nutmeg, salt and pepper and beat the potato mixture with a wooden spoon until light and fluffy. Garnish with parsley and serve immediately.

vegetable rösti

ingredients

serves 4

1 carrot, peeled and grated
1 courgette, grated
1 sweet potato, peeled and grated
8 spring onions, finely chopped
   or shredded
1 egg white, beaten
2 tsp extra virgin olive oil
pepper

method

1 Mix all the vegetables together, season to taste with pepper and stir in the egg white. Using clean hands, form the mixture into 8 small patties. Press them firmly together.

2 Heat the oil in a non-stick frying pan and cook the patties, in batches, over a gentle heat for 5–6 minutes, or until golden. Turn over halfway through the cooking time and press down with the back of a spatula. Serve immediately.

cauliflower cheese

ingredients

serves 4

1 cauliflower, trimmed and cut
    into florets
40 g/1½ oz butter
40 g/1½ oz plain flour
450 ml/16 fl oz milk
115 g/4 oz Cheddar cheese,
    finely grated
pinch of ground nutmeg
1 tbsp grated Parmesan cheese
salt and pepper

method

1 Cook the cauliflower in a saucepan of boiling water for 4–5 minutes. Drain and place in a baking dish.

2 Melt the butter in a saucepan over a medium heat and stir in the flour. Cook for 1 minute, stirring constantly, then remove from the heat and add the milk gradually until smooth. Return to a low heat, bring to the boil and simmer until the sauce is thick and creamy. Remove from the heat and stir in the Cheddar cheese and nutmeg. Season to taste with salt and pepper.

3 Preheat the grill. Pour the cheese sauce over the cauliflower, sprinkle over the Parmesan cheese and place under the grill to brown. Serve.

apple & blackberry crumble

ingredients

serves 6

450 g/1 lb cooking apples
450 g/1 lb blackberries
115 g/4 oz caster sugar
4 tbsp water
cream, for serving

crumble topping

175 g/6 oz wholemeal flour
85 g/3 oz unsalted butter
85 g/3 oz soft light brown sugar
1 tsp mixed spice

method

1 Preheat the oven to 190°C/375°F/Gas Mark 5.

2 Prepare the apples by cutting them into quarters, then peeling and coring them. Thinly slice them into an ovenproof dish. Add the blackberries and then stir in the sugar. Pour over the water.

3 Make the crumble topping by placing the flour in a mixing bowl and rubbing in the butter until the mixture resembles breadcrumbs. Stir in the sugar and mixed spice. Spread the crumble evenly over the fruit and press down lightly.

4 Put the dish on a baking sheet and bake in the centre of the preheated oven for 25–30 minutes, until the crumble is golden brown. Serve with cream.

creamy rice pudding

ingredients

serves 4

butter, for greasing
85 g/3 oz sultanas, plus extra
    to decorate
5 tbsp caster sugar
90 g/3¼ oz pudding rice
1.2 litres/2 pints milk
1 tsp vanilla extract
finely grated rind of 1 large lemon
pinch of ground nutmeg
chopped pistachio nuts,
    to decorate

method

1 Preheat the oven to 160°C/325°F/Gas Mark 3. Grease an 850-ml/1½-pint ovenproof dish.

2 Put the sultanas, sugar and rice into a mixing bowl, then stir in the milk and vanilla extract. Transfer to the prepared dish, sprinkle over the lemon rind and nutmeg, then bake in the preheated oven for 2½ hours.

3 Remove from the oven and transfer to individual serving bowls. Decorate with sultanas and chopped pistachio nuts and serve.

chocolate mousse

ingredients

serves 4

300 g/10½ oz plain chocolate
1½ tbsp unsalted butter
1 tbsp brandy
4 eggs, separated

method

1 Break the chocolate into small pieces and place in a heatproof bowl set over a pan of gently simmering water. (Make sure that the base of the bowl does not touch the water.) Add the butter and melt with the chocolate, stirring, until smooth. Remove from the heat, stir in the brandy and leave to cool slightly. Add the egg yolks and beat until smooth.

2 In a separate bowl, whisk the egg whites until stiff peaks have formed, then fold them into the chocolate mixture. Spoon the mixture into 4 small serving bowls and level the surfaces. Transfer to the refrigerator and chill for at least 4 hours, until set.

3 Take the mousse out of the refrigerator and serve.

quick tiramisù

ingredients

serves 4

225 g/8 oz mascarpone cheese
  or full-fat soft cheese
1 egg, separated
2 tbsp natural yogurt
2 tbsp caster sugar
2 tbsp dark rum
2 tbsp cold strong black coffee
8 sponge fingers
2 tbsp grated plain chocolate

method

1 Put the mascarpone cheese, egg yolk and yogurt in a large bowl and beat together until smooth.

2 Whisk the egg white in a separate bowl until stiff peaks have formed, then whisk in the sugar and gently fold into the cheese mixture. Divide half the mixture between 4 sundae glasses.

3 Mix the rum and coffee together in a shallow dish. Dip the sponge fingers into the rum mixture, break them in half, or into smaller pieces if necessary, and divide between the glasses.

4 Stir any remaining coffee mixture into the remaining cheese mixture and divide between the glasses.

5 Sprinkle with the grated chocolate. Serve immediately or cover and chill in the refrigerator until required.

index